Volcanoes and Thermal Springs

NEW HOLLAND

First English language edition published in 1998 by
New Holland (Publishers) Ltd
London - Cape Town - Sydney - Singapore

24 Nutford Place
London W1H 6DQ
United Kingdom

80 McKenzie Street
Cape Town 8001
South Africa

3/2 Aquatic Drive
Frenchs Forest, NSW 2086
Australia

First published in 1997 in The Netherlands as
Vulkanen en Thermische bronnen by
Holding B. van Dobbenburgh bv, Nieuwkoop,
The Netherlands
Written by: Peter J. Meijer
Translated from the Dutch by: K.M.M. Hudson-Brazenall

ISBN 1-85368-628-x

Editorial direction: D-Books International Publishing
Design: Meijster Design bv
Cover design: M.T. van Dobbenburgh

Reproduction by Unifoto International Pty, Ltd

Technical Production by D-Books International
Publishing/Agora United Graphic Services bv

Printed and bound in Spain by Egedsa, Sabadell

CONTENTS

PHOTO CREDITS

Introduction

Vulcanism and thermal springs have much in common as they both result from hot molten rock welling-up from the depths of the earth.

The first section of this book deals with examples of vulcanism. The word vulcanism is derived from Vulcanus who, according to Roman mythology, was the god of fire and smithery and had his forge under Mount Etna. Volcanoes are found in places where molten rock bursts through the earth's crust and flows out on to the surface. An eruption is a very impressive natural phenomenon causing enormous destruction on the one hand and, on the other, providing fertile new soils suitable for agriculture. This is the reason why many volcanic regions are densely populated, a good example being the island of Java in the Indonesian archipelago.

In addition to vulcanism, other phenomena are caused by the enormous pressures and extreme temperatures that occur inside the earth, thus heating gas or water that is within the earth's crust so much that it expands and is pushed upwards with great force. On the earth's surface, this gives rise to hot springs, smoke plumes and geysers; it is these and other thermal activities that are described in the second part of the book.

1 Vulcanism

Inside the earth

If we were able to take a look at the structure of the inside of the earth we would see the following: the interior of the earth consists of hot material surrounded by a thin layer, the CRUST. The crust is the part of the earth on which we live. The earth's crust and the uppermost section of the mantle are together called the LITHOSPHERE. Litho is derived from the Greek word for stone. The lithosphere is broken up into plates that according to the theory of PLATE TECTONICS move past, away or towards each other. The speed of this movement is not usually greater than one to ten centimetres per year.

The island of Lanzarote consists of volcanic rock and the conical mountains are clearly recognizable as volcanoes.

However, the plates are not continually in motion. Below the crust lies the MANTLE, which is divided into the upper and lower mantle. The mantle is composed of hard rock. In the centre of the earth lies the CORE, which is composed of a hard inner core and fluid outer core. Inside the earth high temperatures and high pressure are the norm.

Magma and lava

The heat inside the earth arises through the natural decay of radioactive elements. In some places, this results in material becoming so hot that it becomes fluid or even gaseous. This material is called magma. Just as when water boils, the magma bubbles upwards to where it is held back by the earth's crust. In certain places it breaks through the faults in the crust, allowing the hot mass to reach the earth's surface and let the heat escape. Processes which are associated with the welling-up of hot material are collectively called vulcanism.

There are two characteristic kinds of magma. Rhyolitic magma is sticky and viscous and is able to retain gases. It can be compared to semi-fluid dough: easy to shape and not runny.

The second type of magma, basalt, is much less sticky and struggles to hold the gases trapped in it. After volcanic eruptions, the magma that reaches the surface is much more fluid and is called lava. This has an initial temperature of around 1,200 °C and flows in streams, rather like slow rivers, across the countryside. Some lava flows flow so slowly that they can be approached by spectators. (Hawaii, USA).

Types of volcanoes

The word volcano makes one most frequently think of a steep conical hill or mountain with a crater vent from which smoke rises. Although this type of volcano (strato volcano) is common, there are also other kinds of volcanoes. The edges of craters are often unstable and crumble away resulting in the typical crater shape. Many volcanoes form side craters on their flanks.

Pico Veijo, Tenerife, Spain.
The darker material is from a later date.

Volcanoes can be divided into three main types according to their form, size and composition:
1. tephra volcanoes
2. shield volcanoes
3. strato volcanoes

Mount Kilimanjaro is the highest free-standing volcanic top in the world at a height of 5,895 metres. The volcano, in Tanzania, is also called the 'big mountain of the springs.' Many rivers rise here, providing water to the flora and fauna on the plains below.

Popacatapetu, Mexico.

Mount Fuji is one of the best known volcanoes in Japan. As high volcanoes are frequently shrouded in cloud, it is often difficult to see whether fumes are spiralling out of the crater. There are some forty active volcanoes in Japan, which according to tradition are fed by an underground dragon.

△Seen here from the south, the Mount Ngauruhoe volcano (New Zealand) reaches a height of 2,287 metres.

◁Tenerife and the other Canary Islands were created entirely through vulcanism. The islands lie above a so-called 'hot spot', a place in the earth's mantle that is hotter than the rest of the mantle.

▷Vesuvius, in Italy, was responsible for the destruction of Pompeii in 79 AD. The eruption of Vesuvius was unexpected; no-one actually knew that the mountain, whose sides were covered in vineyards, was volcanically active. The town was engulfed in a thick layer of volcanic ash.

Mount Rainier (Washington, USA) is, at 4,392 metres, the highest mountain in the state of Washington. Indians who lived in the area for thousands of years, were afraid of the volcano. No-one dared to climb to the top, and people only hunted on the lower slopes. They believed that a monstrous spirit lived in Mount Rainier that sometimes tormented the Indians by spouting its venom.

Tephra volcanoes

Tephra volcanoes are easily recognised by their steep-sided 30° slopes. The material that is released after an explosive eruption mostly lands close to the crater. The steepness of the slope is never more than 33° due to the force of gravity, and tephra volcanoes rarely exceed more than 300 metres in height. A tephra volcano is composed of magma and associated rocks. The material expelled from a volcano in either fluid or solid form is called pyroclastic fragments. The deposit of loose material built up is known as a pyroclastic deposit or tephra. Examples of tephra volcanoes can be found in the Eiffel (Germany).

Shield volcanoes

Shield volcanoes are composed of solidified lava flows and are much flatter in shape than the tephra and strato volcanoes. They are broad, gently sloping cones. As a result of the relatively high fluidity of the magma, the lava flows spread out over a wide area during eruptions. The slope of a shield volcano is often less than 10°; this is because the lava does not pile up around the central vent, as is the case with a tephra volcano, but spreads out over a wider area. Moreover, the lava does not always flow only from the central vent, but may also flow from a side vent in the flanks of the volcano. Hawaii is built up from a number of shield volcanoes. These volcanoes are composed of basalt layers. Shield volcanoes can cover vast areas, for example the Mauna Kea on Hawaii, which is mentioned in the Guinness Book of Records as the largest mountain in the world. This volcano comprises some 16,000 cubic kilometres of massive rock. Mauna Kea is much higher and more voluminous than Mount Everest in the Himalayas, yet there is a remarkable difference between these two giants. Mauna Kea has no steep slopes and the peak, in contrast to that of Mount Everest (8,847 metres), only rises to about 4,200 metres above sea level, whilst the rest of the giant, which is slightly more than 10 kilometres in height, all lies below the surface of the Pacific.

Strato volcanoes

Strato volcanoes are the most common type of volcano; they are composed of solidified lava flows alternating with layers of pyroclastic material. The solidified lava flows act like a protective blanket for the layers of loose

In the middle of North Island, New Zealand, lies Tongariro National Park. In this rugged wilderness lie the volcanoes Mount Ngauruhoe and Mount Ruapehu, the latter of which was still active in the autumn of 1995.

Over time, precipitation can cause lakes to form on some volcanoes. Both crater lakes and snow cover on a volcano can cause large mud flows (also called 'lahars') during a subsequent eruption.Tongario National Park, North Island, New Zealand.

In the winter, snow lies on the slopes of Mount Ruapehu (New Zealand).
An eruption in 1995 caused huge mud flows and avalanches.

pyroclastic material. The steepness of the slope is intermediate between that of a tephra and that of a shield volcano. A good example of this type of volcano can be found along the 'ring of fire' in Mount Fujiyama (3,776 metres), Japan. This dormant volcano has an almost perfect cone shape.

Geographical location

More than 1,500 active volcanoes can be found scattered around the world, but they are not always visible: if they are on the sea bed, then they are often fully under water. Volcanoes occur where the magma forces its way through the earth's crust, usually where there are faults. It finally reaches the surface and spreads out over the land or sea bed. The continents move on at least six

Escaping gases form a hazard on Mount Ruapehu. Depending on the wind direction and speed, the danger could spread in different directions. People in the direct vicinity must always be aware of the dangers of gas clouds.

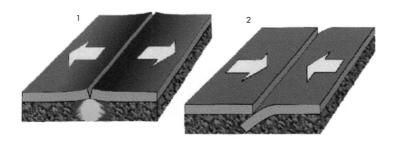

1. Where the earth's plates move apart, the space produced fills with magma and volcanoes are created. Examples of this are the volcanic ridges in the middle of the oceans.
2. When the plates move towards each other, usually one plate dips underneath the other. At a certain depth, the rock of the dipping plate will melt and return to the surface as magma.

High in the Andes, in Ecuador, lies Cotopaxi Quito. At 5,897 metres high, it is the highest active volcano in the world.

large tectonic plates. The boundaries of these are marked by regions of high earthquake activity and by strings of volcanoes. This movement is very, very slow: at most only a few centimetres a year. Some plates move away from each other and in the space between them, magma wells up, forming a new crust and a ridge of volcanoes. Such ridges can be found in the middle of the oceans. Iceland, a large island almost wholly composed of volcanic material

(basalt), is part of the Mid-Atlantic Ridge that sticks out above the water. Vulcanism occurs not only along the edges of a plate, but can also occur within a plate. These upwellings are caused by active chambers, so-called hot spots that produce enormous quantities of magma. If the magma breaks through the crust, then volcanoes can be formed, such as on the Galapagos Islands, the Canary Islands and in East Africa.

Famous eruptions

Large volcanic eruptions often have very far-reaching consequences for mankind and the environment. Famous eruptions include those of Vesuvius (79 AD, Italy), Krakatau (1883, Indonesia), Mont Pelée (1902, Martinique) Katmai (1912, USA), Mount St. Helens (1980, USA) and Mount Pinatubo (1991, Philippines).

The eruption of Vesuvius, on 24 August in the year 79 AD came completely unexpectedly for the inhabitants of the Roman towns of Pompeii and Herculeum. Hot ash rained down on Pompeii for hours and the town was buried under a layer of ash several metres thick. In the seaside town of Herculeum, to the west of Naples, almost no ash fell, but tons of volcanic mud, which swept down the mountain, buried the town.

In later years Vesuvius, with its green hillsides and vineyards, was considered dormant since no activity had been observed in 800 years. In 1860, under the leadership of Guiseppe Fiorelli, the first systematic excavations of Pompeii were started. Bodily remains were found which were so well preserved that the frightened expressions could still be seen on people's faces.

The eruption of Mount St. Helens (USA) on 18 May 1980 claimed the lives of 57 people. It was one of the most massive explosions of the century. Three cubic kilometres of rock were blasted off the mountain at a speed of 215 kilometres per hour. A huge column of volcanic ash shot into the air, reaching a height of 25 kilometres within three-quarters of a hour. Three days later, carried on the wind, the cloud of ash reached New York, some 4,000 kilometres away.

The landscape in the vicinity of Mount St.Helens has been completely changed by the eruption of 1980. The once thickly-wooded region with its attractive lakes, has been completely transformed into a lunar landscape.

The eruption of Krakatau, the volcanic island between Java and Sumatra, took place in 1883. The explosion had a force equivalent to that of several atom bombs. Two-thirds of the island disappeared, comparable to 18 cubic kilometres of rock. Material was blasted more than 16 kilometres up into the stratosphere and spread over 765,000 square kilometres, leaving some places in darkness for more than two and a half days. Within 15 days the ash had circled the earth. Dust particles remained in the atmosphere for more than two years and were the cause of many red sunsets. The pressure waves following the eruption caused huge masses of water to move. These huge tidal waves, called tsunamis, hit the coasts of the surrounding islands, in particular Java and Sumatra, causing some 30,000 people to die.

The eruption of Mont Pelée in 1902 on Martinique was also unexpected. After 50 years of inactivity, the volcano burst into life. St Pierre, the capital of this Caribbean island, lies eight kilometres from the volcano, but was devastated by the hot cloud of ash, which formed during the eruption. The cloud rushed down the mountain at about 200 kilometres per hour. The cloud consisted of hot ash particles that floated on the gases which had been released. These gases acted like a cushion, on which the hot material slid downwards. Such an ash cloud is called 'nuée ardente', literally a burning cloud. All but two of the 30,000 inhabitants of the capital died. One of the survivors was a prisoner locked up in a dungeon.

The eruption of Mount St. Helens in 1980 in the State of Washington in the north-west of the USA was, like so many eruptions, preceded by small earthquakes and an increase in pressure under the volcano. This caused the mountain to expand in fits and starts on its northern slopes at a rate of 1.5 metres a day. By continuing to study the expansion carefully, the scientists were able to predict the eruption extremely well. The number of victims was limited by timely precautions, which meant that people were evacuated from within a 30 kilometres radius of the mountain.

On 18 May 1980 at 8.32 in the morning the volcano erupted. The northern flank and the top were blown away completely. Within 15 seconds, 3 cubic kilometres of rock

The Mount St. Helens explosion took place from the side of the volcano. A huge hole was blown out of the side of the mountain. Mount St. Helens is once again quiet, but its appearance has been radically altered. The explosion created a crater 3 kilometres long, 1.5 kilometres wide and 700 metres deep. The top of the mountain is now 430 metres lower.

Apart from a profusion of paddy-fields, Indonesia is also rich in volcanoes. Volcanic soils contain many minerals and are therefore very fertile. Many paddy-fields are fed by rainwater that runs off the mountains.

was blasted off the mountain and down the northern slope at a speed of 215 kilometres per hour, after which the magma began to spurt out of the mountain. For 30 hours, exploding gases shot lava and ash vertically into the atmosphere. A huge mushroom-shaped ash cloud quickly formed, reaching a height of 25 kilometres after only a quarter of an hour. The cloud of ash, which in some places caused the daylight to be obscured, was carried by the wind, and traces of the ash could be found 330 kilometres from the volcano. A horizontal shock wave travelling at the speed of sound (1,224 kilometres per hour) destroyed everything it met. Within a few seconds of the eruption, everything within a radius of 10 kilometres was stripped of its vegetation and the top layer of soil was removed. Within a radius of 30 kilometres, trees were snapped like matchsticks. The vulcanologist, David A. Johnston, who had taken up position at a distance of 10 kilometres, was only able to scream through his radio, 'Vancouver, Vancouver. This is it!', before the connection broke and 63 people, including David A. Johnston, were killed.

A volcanic eruption takes place.

Most of the material in the underlying reservoir is discharged.

Due to the weight of the overlying rocks the volcano collapses, forming a large crater.

In the course of time, rainwater fills the crater, forming a crater lake.

Eruption of Semeru, East Java, Indonesia. Volcanic eruptions and collapsed craters have created a landscape of great natural beauty.

A lonely church tower is all that is left standing in the neighbourhood of Paracutin, Mexico, after lava buried the landscape.

Gigantic mud flows inundated a large area, carrying houses, machinery and trees for several kilometres. One train was later found seven kilometres from the railway line. One house was carried for several kilometres and finally came to rest on someone else's property. For years there was a legal wrangle as to who exactly owned that house!

What was once a rural tourist area, was, in a matter of seconds, reshaped into a ghostly landscape consisting of a huge mush of mud and ash.

The eruption of Katmai, in Alaska, USA, took place in 1912. Measured on the basis of the amount of material expelled, this was the largest eruption this century. Vast amounts of hot, fine material were thrown out and, carried by volcanic gases and steam, were spread almost instantaneously. Remote areas of Alaska were covered in enormous quantities of ash, in some places forming a layer more than 100 metres thick.

The eruption of Pinatubo on the Philippines took place in June 1991 after six centuries of dormancy. During the eruption, Pinatubo produced seven cubic kilometres of ash. The eruption was accompanied by a mud flow, caused by heavy rainfall on the fresh ash layer, which swept away roads, bridges and whole villages in its path. Although the eruption had been well predicted and many inhabitants had been evacuated from the surrounding area, 300 people still lost their lives and 400,000 were made homeless. This was mostly caused by roofs caving in under the weight of the thick layer of ash covering them. The rescue work was hampered because it remained dark during the day. A large ash cloud was released into the atmosphere and had travelled around the world within three weeks.

The ring of fire

Around the Pacific Ocean lies the 'ring of fire', formed by the volcanoes on the edges of various plates. The ring runs along the west coast of both South and North America, via Alaska, down the eastern side of the Asian continent and on to New Zealand. Most of the world's volcanoes lie on this ring.

Cotopaxi Quito, which lies high in the Andes mountain chain, forms part of this ring of fire. At 5,897 metres high, it is the highest active volcano in the world, and whilst its top is covered with snow at present, at some point in the future, hot magma will flow out again. In the vicinity of Cotopaxi lies Chiborazo, an extinct volcano 6,310 metres high, but this too, given its position on the equator, is also a record breaker. The top of this volcano is actually further from the centre of the earth than the 8,848 metre high peak of Mount Everest, because the earth is not a perfect sphere but bulges at the equator. In Alaska, the Valley of the Ten Thousand Smokes, containing the Katmai volcano, also constitutes part of the ring of fire.

Areas in Iceland where lava no longer flows, are covered with moss. Because the climate is cold and inclement, almost no other vegetation grows here.

The Colorado region of Bolivia.
Trees do not grow here in the warm
soils. On the left in the foreground,
several pools can be seen where
gases are bubbling up. The gases,
which sometimes contain dangerous
substances, emanate from the
underlying magma body.

Fumes still hang above this crater landscape. Some gases are heavier than air and they linger just above the surface. In former times, vulcanologists often used to take dogs with them on their study trips. The dogs would bark when they smelt unsavoury gases.

These craters were formed when lava still flowed here. Hot material and gases escaped from the holes, after which the ground sank a little leaving the shape that is now visible.

26

Volcanoes and the climate

Large volcanic eruptions influence the climate as a result of the huge quantities of material that are thrown several kilometres into the atmosphere. These form a mushroom-shaped cloud that hangs above the volcano and consists of gases (including water vapour, carbon dioxide and sulphur dioxide) and fine dust particles. Millions of tons of gas may be released into the stratosphere. From the sulphur dioxide, tiny sulphur particles called aerosols are produced, which are capable of reflecting and partially absorbing light, resulting in only some of the sun's rays actually reaching the earth's surface. It is then a little colder for a short period. This

On Tenerife (Canary Islands) the structure of the lava flow can still be seen in the landscape. A crust formed on the hot lava which then took on a scaly appearance.

This crater on the island of Lanzarote (Canary Islands) is filled with ash and other fragments, called cinders. Small bushes grow In the holes, bringing some life to this otherwise rather dead environment.

Lanzarote. The edges of a lava flow can still be vaguely distinguished. To the left lies a sputter cone. As a result of the sputtering the lava is thrown up and deposited in layers, one on top of the other, forming a small cone.

Seen from above, this region can be clearly divided into 'old' and 'new' lava. The old lava is lighter in colour and has been colonised in places by vegetation. The relatively younger material is much blacker. In some places, the 'old' rock has been engulfed by the 'new' lava.

▷Magma welling up causes cracks in the crust. A long row of craters, created when the Lagagíga volcano erupted in 1783, are the result of this. This was the most catastrophic eruption ever in Iceland.

happened when the Tambora volcano erupted in Indonesia in 1815. The following year is still frequently referred to as the 'year without a summer'. The dust in the high layers of the atmosphere continued to ensure that the sun's rays were deflected whilst also causing a red glow at sunset for several years. This phenomenon also occurred after the eruptions of Krakatau

28

in Indonesia in 1883 and of Pinatubo in the Philippines in 1991. Vulcanologists are not yet able to reliably demonstrate how great the influence of volcanic eruptions on climatic changes can be, since many factors play a role in such changes. However, most scientists would agree that major eruptions do influence climate, and it is only the degree to which this occurs that is still subject to discussion.

Some meteorologists have linked the following weather phenomena with the Pinatubo eruption: a temperature fall of 0.5 °C the following year with a particularly cold and snowy winter in New Zealand, several large hurricanes, including hurricaines Andrew and Iniki, and the heavy rainfall in the Mid-West of the USA in 1993.

Gases rise from the vents in the crater of this volcano. It is usually water vapour, but sometimes poisonous gases like carbon dioxide or sulphur fumes also escape. The yellow patches low down in the crater are the result of the deposition of sulphur-bearing minerals.

Caldera of the Nyira Gonga volcano on the eastern border of Congo. Within the caldera, a second crater has formed which is smoking dangerously and is apparently still volcanically active.

Where volcanoes are no longer active, craters sometimes fill with water, from rain or melted snow. The lake in the foreground has broken through the crater rim, but the circular shape of the former crater is still clearly recognizable.

The steep cliffs of the caldera ring the sparkling water of Crater Lake in the state of Oregon (USA). With a depth of more than 600 metres, this is the deepest lake in the United States. Only six lakes in the world are deeper. Crater Lake was formed when the cone of Mount Mazuma collapsed. This dangerous volcano was active thousands of years ago.

Calderas and crater lakes

Volcanoes typically have dormant and active periods and if a volcano has been inactive for more than 100 years then it is classified as extinct. Volcanoes give the landscape a distinctive appearance: high tops are usually covered with snow and fumes rise from some volcanoes. Each year there are about 40 eruptions worldwide.

Following a major eruption, a volcano may be unstable as a result of the disappearance of a large quantity of material. The fault-rich rock at the top

Lake Quilotoa is a crater lake close to the city of Quito in Ecuador, in the Andes Mountains. The volcanoes in the Andes are part of the 'ring of fire'. Some are still active but many are extinct. The craters of the latter are often filled with water.

Lake Turkana, in northern Kenya, was formed after large faults arose in the earth's crust in the volcanic region. The lake is encircled by dull grey lava boulders. In this landscape the only animal species to survive are those that are millions of years old, such as snakes, crocodiles and scorpions.

collapses inwards towards the magma chamber, forming a circular depression with steep walls. A clear crater shape is then visible which, if it measures several kilometres in diameter, is called a caldera. Over time, calderas of non-active volcanoes fill up with snow and rainwater, forming crater lakes in which new craters may form during later eruptions. A good example of a crater lake is the aptly named Crater Lake in southern Oregon, USA, which was formed more than 7,000 years ago following a gigantic eruption of Mount Mazama. This crater formed after a vast quantity of magma had flowed out of the volcano with a crater lake of extreme dimensions the result; Crater Lake has a diameter of 10 kilometres and is up to 600 metres deep in places.

Crater lakes can also be the cause of disasters, as demonstrated by Lake Nyos in Cameroon. Lake Nyos lies in the crater of an extinct volcano and, on 21 August 1986 following a thunderous noise, a huge cloud of poisonous gas welled up from the crater. Since the gas that had been released was heavier than air, it was unable to rise and therefore poured into the valleys leaving about 1,650 people dead in its wake.

Spreading flows of lava can be spectacularly vast. A wide river of lava flows from the Nyira Gonga volcano (Congo). Fortunately, most flows are not fast, so man and animals can often avoid them.

Mud flows

Mud flows, so-called lahars, can cause immense damage. Mud flows that followed the relatively small eruption of the Ruiz volcano (Mexico) in 1985 were caused by the melting snow on its slopes, and about 25,000 people were engulfed by the waves of mud and boulders. When Mount Ruapehu

(New Zealand) erupted in 1995, huge mud and snow flows followed; fortunately these occurred in a thinly populated area.

The Icelandic volcano Bararbunga lies below Europe's largest glacier, Vatnajökull (Water Glacier). The eruption of the volcano on the north-western side of the glacier, at the beginning of October 1996, led to an enormous flood on 5 November 1996. The volcanic activity caused a huge

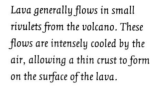

◁Watching active lava flows at night provides an extra dimension, especially when small explosions are still occurring. These can throw small fragments of glowing lava tens of metres into the air.

Lava generally flows in small rivulets from the volcano. These flows are intensely cooled by the air, allowing a thin crust to form on the surface of the lava.

Black and dangerously hot aptly describes the landscape around an active volcano. In the background stands the conical shape of Pu'u O'o, which lies on the flanks of Kilauea (Hawaii). Since 1983, lava has streamed almost continuously from Kilauea at this point.

Volcanic islands can also become considerably larger due to huge eruptions. The lava flows off the island into the ocean. In this way, several square kilometres may be added to the land area. The smoke plumes here clearly show where the hot underground lava flows meet the cold sea water.

Usually the lava flows into the ocean below sea level, but sometimes this happens on land, allowing us to witness the battle between water and fire. The water evaporates instantly on the lava, which has a temperature of 1,100 oC, so that it appears to be losing the battle, but the ground is very unstable. Chunks regularly break off the coast due to the constant battering of the waves as the sea takes back what belongs to it.

quantity of meltwater to build up in Grimsvatn, the lake that lies under the glacier. Within only a few days the level of the lake had already risen by 20 metres and when it had filled up to overflowing, the pressure of the water forced up the icecap, allowing 45,000 cubic metres of water per second to escape. A gigantic flood wave was the result, causing about US$15 million in damage. This flood washed away a ten kilometre stretch of the only road along the south coast and destroyed bridges, electricity and telephone lines, and anything else that stood in its path.

Lava products

If a volcano is active, then small eruptions may occur repeatedly at short intervals, filling the crater with red-hot, molten rock. If gas bubbles escape from this hot mass then it can begin to sputter. As a result of the cooling of the lava exposed to the air, a section of the lava lake can acquire a thin crust, and since this solidified crust is heavier than the underlying material it will sink back into the lake. The products tossed out by the sputtering rock are called pyroclastic fragments, a word derived from the Greek words 'pyros' and 'klastos' which mean, respectively, fire and fragment.

The glass-like structure and its black colour are both characteristic of rapidly cooled pyroclastic material. These fragments are called bombs, lapilli and ash, depending upon their sizes. One example of volcanic glass is obsidian, which was even used in the Stone Age to manufacture weapons and tools. Nowadays it is used as a decorative stone. Pumice is also a pyroclast: it is a piece of stone that once contained a lot of gas. After the gas

A hole in the crust, a so-called 'sky-light', acts like a window through which the lava flow can be observed. Scientists use these holes to determine the speed of the flow, by throwing a large stick into a sky-light and measuring how long it takes to appear in another hole.

Large lava flows can move quite rapidly. A river of glowing, hot lava can achieve speeds of up to several tens of kilometres per hour. The colour of the material is an indicator of the temperature. The yellow patches in this lava flow in Congo are the hottest. The black crusts that form on the flow are cooler.

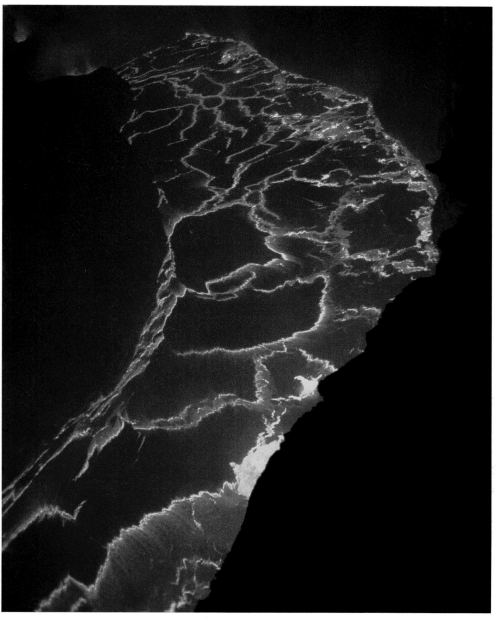

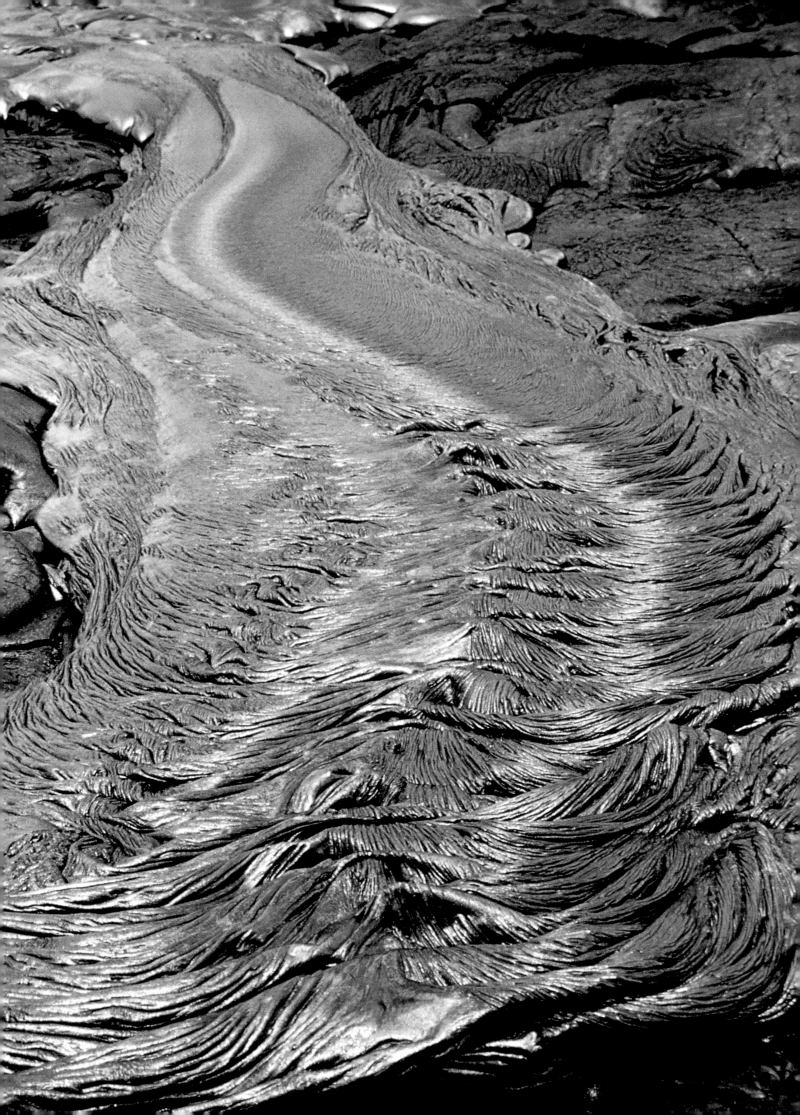

◁△Basaltic lava takes two different forms as it flows out: ropy lava and block lava. As a flow moves forward a thin crust develops on the lava. As a result of the pressure from within the lava, the crust breaks open and fresh lava flows out again. A crust again forms on top and the process repeats itself. With the new lava bursting through, a folded crust is formed, which, when it solidifies looks a lot like coils of rope: hence the name ropy lava.

escaped and the stone solidified, myriads of holes were left giving the stone the appearance of a sponge. The many, hollow spaces make the stone so light that it can float on water. Whenever new magma is continually brought to the surface, the hot material will flow through the cracks in the crater walls and down the slopes of the mountain. Normally these flows are no wider than a couple of metres but with larger scale eruptions they can be ten times wider and, with a few exceptions, they flow so slowly that people and animals can avoid them. A river of lava, however, has no set route and forces its destructive way through fields, houses, roads and bridges.

Block lava consists of very irregular jagged blocks, with sharp edges. Despite the fact that these are of the same composition as pahoehoe, they look totally different.

39

Gas bubbles escaping from lava cause the hot mass to sputter. The materials thrown out by the sputtering lava, are known as pyroclasts.This word is derived from the Greek words 'pyros' and 'klastos' ,which mean respectively, fire and fragment.

When lava flows over a steep hillside, a sort of waterfall of lava develops, a 'lavafall'. At its base a small lava lake forms, which greedily absorbs the falling lumps.

The Kilauea volcano on Hawaii has been very active in the last few decades, with magma flowing out through fissures in the volcano about halfway up the slopes, from the magma reservoir that lies a few kilometres under the crater. Most of the entrapped gases dissipate in this manner and as a result, the basaltic magma is not very explosive. The lava from Kilauea flows down to the ocean in small rivers across an area several kilometres wide. A thin crust forms on top due to the cooling of the lava, creating small tunnels through which the lava flows. If a tunnel gets blocked, the hot material then bursts out through the crust. This produces some spectacular images, particularly after sunset, when the red glow of the lava can be seen through

Lava flows destroy everything in their paths. Trees catch fire immediately and lava crusts form around the trees. Once a tree has (partially) burned down or has fallen over, then this crust is all that is left behind. This is called a tree-molt. The section of the trunk in the foreground has been left unburnt because of lack of oxygen; only the outside is charred.

all the nooks and crannies. It is therefore not surprising that such an impressive region with 'live' vulcanism attracts many tourists.

There are two types of basalt forms: ropy lava and block lava. Ropy lava forms when a crust on the hot mass repeatedly breaks open under pressure from the material inside. When fresh lava streams out, this process repeats itself, leaving a threadlike or folded surface, which, after solidifying looks like the coils of a rope.

Block lava is formed when the lava flow pushes the solidified material ahead of itself, forming irregular angular blocks with sharp corners. It has much the same composition as ropy lava, but looks totally different and ropy lava can, whilst flowing, change to block lava. The Hawaiian name for these lavas is used internationally: pahoehoe (pronounced pa-hoy-hoy) for ropy lava, whilst block lava is called 'aa' (pronounced ah-ah), an onomatopoeic sound describing a Hawaiian walking over the viciously sharp rocks.

Tsunamis

When volcanoes erupt in the sea, pressure waves are created, which move at great speed. In shallow seas this generates huge tidal waves. When such a wave hits the coast, the effect is often catastrophic. It has nothing to do with ebb and flood tides and is called a tsunami by scientists. Tsunamis often occur after earthquakes and volcanic eruptions around the 'ring of fire'. Their affects can often be felt on coasts many thousands of miles away, like the frequently affected Japanese coast, whilst they can also cause immense damage in the Philippines and in the Indonesian Archipelago.

Science and volcanoes

All over the world, volcanoes are being carefully studied, not only for their scientific interest, but also in order to be able to predict their eruptions more accurately and thus limit the damage caused by them.

Earthquakes also form part of the discipline of vulcanism. The shock waves associated with the upward thrust of the magma, are an indication of the activity taking place at great depth. Whilst most shocks are small and barely perceptible, seismic instruments register all the earthquakes in the ground and increasing intensity and frequency is an indication of what is to come. The changes noted in the chemical composition of the volcanic gases is a further indicator, and these gases are regularly sampled and investigated for this reason. Movements of the flanks of a volcano are also carefully monitored, since a rise in the level of the ground often indicates an impending eruption, as with Mount St Helens. Through constant measurement and analysis, scientists continue to gain more insights into the phenomenon of vulcanism.

In the foreground a seven metre thick layer of basaltic lava can be seen. When basalt cools, hexagonal columns are formed. This layer now appears to have vertical stripes.

2 Thermal Activity

The chapter on vulcanism describes the effects of magma extruding onto the surface. However, when the magma does not break through the earth's crust, the molten rock can still cause effects which manifest themselves on the surface. This is especially true when the magma lies close to the surface and at a relatively shallow depth, giving off heat to its surroundings. Various processes occur as a result, including the heating of any water or gas which is in the ground. Hot water, steam and hot gases are forced up and escape through cracks and faults in the earth's crust, dissolving and transporting minerals on the way. These substances are later deposited in upper soil layers or dumped on the surface, resulting in rock deposits with high mineral concentrations. In some cases, these deposits, known as ores, can be economically extracted.

As a result of the movement of magma through the mantle, long faults occur in the earth's crust. Along these fault lines, gases and fumes are able to escape at the surface. Fault systems in volcanic regions are responsible for the supply and drainage of water and gas. It is through this transport system that thermal activity takes place.

Holes in the ground from where fumes drift into the atmosphere are called fumaroles. The most common component of the fumes is water vapour, but carbon dioxide and sulphurous fumes are also emitted. The temperature of the gases varies between 50 oC and 600 oC. Fumaroles can either discharge gases continuously or periodically, depending on the underground supply system.

The phenomena related to the heat given off by the magma are called thermal activity. Some examples of thermal activity are thermal springs, geysers, steam holes (fumaroles) and hot mud pools. Thermal activity occurs particularly on or around volcanoes, above the warm magma chamber, and although the volcanoes themselves may often have been extinct for a long time, thermal activity is still present. For example, it is 10,000 years ago since the last volcanic eruption took place near the LacherSee in Germany, but carbon dioxide gas is still venting from the ground.

The most extensive and best known areas of thermal activity are in Iceland, New Zealand and in Yellowstone Park in the United States.

Man makes use of this thermal activity in various ways:
- minerals are exploited, provided these are deposited in sufficiently high concentrations
- hot gases, particularly steam, are used to generate electricity in thermal power stations
- springs, warmed by deeper-lying layers, are used to heat towns and greenhouses, or used to supply swimming pools with warm water
- regions with thermal activity are great tourist attractions.

Ground water that lies in the deeper strata of the earth's crust, is heated and starts to rise. In porous, non-consolidated layers this takes place quite easily, but in harder bedrock this movement can only take place along faults and fissures in the bedrock. This results in a build-up of pressure in the steaming hot water, which finally spouts out on to the surface.

Supply of water

Thermal activity results mainly in water and carbon dioxide being forced out of the earth's crust. At times, the water is forced out as steam, at other times as hot water. Water and carbon dioxide (CO_2) together represent nearly 98% of the entire thermal production, with the remainder consisting of sulphur dioxide (SO_2), hydrogen sulphide (H_2S) and hydrogen chloride (HCl).

The majority of the water that rises in warm springs and geysers has been transported from elsewhere in the form of rainwater or melted snow. Rain and snow sink through the porous ground or through cracks in the rocks

◁The Indonesian archipelago consists of thousands of volcanoes. For this reason the land also has many thermal springs.
This river has a yellow-green colour. The water is heavily contaminated with naturally-occurring sulphur from the soil. Such a sulphur-bearing river is poisonous to both man and animals.

Thermal springs can be found in various places on earth. These hot springs often have a volcanic origin, but they can also acquire their warmth in other ways. In general, hot springs are defined as springs where the temperature of the water is higher than that of the human body. Globally, the largest and best known regions with thermal activity are Iceland (left) New Zealand and Yellowstone Park in the United States (below).

until this water reaches a place where it can be warmed by the underlying hot layers. Sometimes the water travels over great distances running through porous layers that are lying at a slight slope. An underlying impervious layer ensures that the water cannot penetrate vertically, forcing sideways transport which occurs when, for instance, a layer of water-bearing sand lies above a clay layer, which is almost impervious. Water-bearing strata, also called aquifers, are the most important suppliers of ground water in thermal regions. In these regions, the earth's crust consists of material with many splits and faults through which the water can easily permeate to great depths. Only a small proportion of the water or steam percolating to the surface actually originates in the magma itself.

Ores

Normally temperatures are extremely high above the centre of a magma body so that the ground water flowing into this area will be heated, causing it to rise and dissipate some of its heat into the surrounding strata. As it rises higher in the crust, this water cools and will, at some distance from the magma body, sink down through the crust and flow back to be re-heated again. Such an underground cycle of water is called a hydrothermal system. Warm water dissolves certain minerals and chemical compounds easily; the hotter the water, the greater the level of minerals which can be dissolved in it. Thus it is possible for hot water to contain up to 35% salts, more than ten times the concentration of sea water. During the upwards transportation of water, certain salts, in particular sulphates, are dissolved out of the surrounding rocks.

The temperature of this spring in Yellowstone Park (USA) is c. 70 oC. The water is heated by superheated steam or other hot gases which bubble up from the depths.

When the water cools off in the upper layers of the crust, its ability to hold salts in solution reduces. The substances that were initially transported in solution by the water precipitate out, and are deposited in the upper layers, thus producing accumulations of certain minerals. However, it is only after thousands of years that such concentrations are large enough to be extracted as ores. Mineralogically, many ores are oxides or sulphides of heavy metals; the most important elements to be extracted are lead, copper, zinc, iron and gold.

Wherever there is volcanic activity, high concentrations of ores are to be found, for example, on the 'ring of fire' in New Guinea and on the west side of North and South America, various large mines are located along these chains of volcanic activity.

Hydrothermal systems are not only found on the land; they are much more commonly found on the sea bed. Along the volcanic oceanic ridges, hot water or steam is pushed up from a great depth, and together with the substances dissolved in it, spouts out through vent holes, rather like black porridge. As soon as the hot material meets the cold sea water, many substances precipitate out and are deposited in the vicinity of the vent hole, building up a kind of chimney around the vent with a high concentration of

It is not difficult to guess how the Blue Star Spring got its name. The star-shaped edge around the clear blue water is accentuated by a clear white deposit of sinter. Yellowstone Park (USA).

minerals. These spouting chimneys are also called 'black smokers'.

Most bodies of ore are formed by hydrothermal systems. They belong to the
so-called endogenous deposits which arise under the influence of magma.
In addition there are also exogenous and metamorphogenic deposits.
Exogenous deposits arise as a result of external influences (air, water, plants
or animals), whereas metamorphogenic deposits arise through changes in
the rock itself (often as a result of high pressure).

Many endogenous ore deposits are found at great depths in the oceans and
are therefore difficult to extract, but where they lie in shallow seas, for
instance around Japan, they are already being mined. In some places, where
the sea bed has risen as a result of geological processes lasting millions of
years, mineral bodies, which were laid down in what was then an ocean,
now form part of the land, for example, in Oman and Cyprus.

Thermal springs and fumaroles

A spring where the water is warmer than the surrounding atmosphere is called a thermal spring. A distinction is made between warm springs and hot springs on the basis of temperature, with warm springs having a water temperature up to 37 °C, and hot springs having a temperature higher than this.

Thermal springs occur all over the world, both in areas with and without volcanic activity, but one pre-condition is that the water must be able to permeate deep enough into the earth's crust to assimilate the heat. In many thermal springs, the water contains large quantities of gases or minerals in solution. Some of these springs are considered to have healing properties, so the water is used for bathing or is drunk as mineral water. Usually it is purified first to remove any dangerous substances, particular in active volcanic areas where the danger is highest.

In cold regions, swimming in thermal springs acquires an added dimension, for the steaming water is even more appealing when the locality is covered in snow. But it is not only humans who make use of warm

◁*Vulcanism on Iceland ensures that the island is continuously under pressure. Earthquakes open long fissures in the crust. Volcanic material, including hot gases and water, spouts out.*

△▷*Wai-O-Tapu Thermal Wonderland, near the town of Rotorua (NewZealand) is home to the famous Champagne Pool. This hot spring was created 900 years ago after a hydrothermal eruption. The Champagne Pool is 60 metres deep and has a circumference of nearly 400 metres. The water has a temperature of more than 70°C. It contains minerals such as gold, silver, thallium, sulphur and arsenic. The last two are responsible for the yellow and orange colours respectively.*

springs. In Japan, there is a famous group of apes that use the warm water in order to survive the winters in the high mountains, when the snow lies like a deep carpet over the ground.

Warm springs are not always healthy for men and animals; they may be dangerous because they may be too warm or contain dissolved heavy metals. Thermal springs are populated by millions of algae that survive in the hot water, causing a wide range of brown, red, orange and green hues with such a rich variation in colour that they provide a very colourful spectacle. Even if only gases and fumes rise from the ground then an area is still considered to be thermally active, but an oppressive,

Landscape with charred trees. Yellowstone Park, USA.

unrealistic atmosphere often lingers over a region of such fuming holes. The holes and fissures through which the fumes rise are called fumaroles, a name derived from the Latin, fumus, which means smoke. Depending on the underground supply system, fumaroles will discharge either continuously or periodically, whilst the composition of the fumes, the temperature of which varies between 50 ° and 600 °C, depends on the temperature. The cooler fumes are mostly water vapour, but they can also contain carbon dioxide and sulphur fumes; and the hot gases have a higher capacity for absorption and are rich in minerals, although they sometimes contain dangerous substances like hydrochloric acid and sulphuric acid.

The substances carried up from great depth precipitate on cooling, often leaving a white deposit of silica (SiO_2), called sinter, around the fumaroles. Yellow tints are caused by sulphurous minerals. The escaping gas is not always observable, although large quantities do disappear into the atmosphere. Measurements have shown that the discharge of carbon dioxide in the direct vicinity of Mount Etna in the periods between eruptions is equivalent to the discharge produced by four large, conventional power generating stations.

Soil layers rich in minerals with bubbling spring. Algae, minerals and bacteria all leave unusually colourful traces behind. Yellowstone Park, USA.

Geysers and geothermal power

When ground water is intensely heated under pressure at great depth, it changes into super-heated steam. When it rises from the depths to meet the outside air, it condenses rapidly and its steaming-hot power becomes visible to the observer.

If extra water is added to this process, then it results in a hot gusher or geyser, a spring that at more or less regular intervals, spouts a stream of

Water can no longer be found in this hot spring. This allows us a clear view of the sinter deposit. This white material consists of SiO_2 (silica). Normally SiO_2 is only soluble in water, but the superheated steam in the depths can absorb it too. When the water cools, sinter is deposited on the rocks, not only on the surface but also in the supply system, thus creating a good, strong, natural water pipeline. Yellowstone Park, USA.

water and steam high into the air. The word geyser comes from the Icelandic word 'geysir'. It is a corruption of an Icelandic verb and means 'upwards force'.

The workings of a geyser are quite complicated, for firstly it needs to have a constant supply of ground water, which ends up in the path of the overheated steam. The cold water then temporarily blocks the upwards path of the steam, resulting in pressure building up in the system and heating of the water lying on top. This water contains a large quantity of dissolved gases, which begin to form small bubbles that get larger as they rise and absorb water in the form of water vapour. The resulting reduction in pressure causes an eruption in the form of a fountain, which lasts until the majority of the hot water has gushed away. After this release, the whole cycle repeats itself.

The temperature of the water in a geyser is usually just below boiling point and eruptions usually last several minutes, although some geysers gush

△▷Ground water that reaches great depths, is heated intensely. The temperature is usually well above boiling point so that the steam becomes superheated. Under great pressure it is then forced to the surface. Superheated steam, which bursts out of the ground, condenses rapidly once it comes into contact with the air. This is how the steaming force becomes visible. A geyser is created when liquid water is added to the superheated steam. Water and steam together shoot sky-high into the air, as with this geyser in Kenya (above) and the Pohutu Geyser (right) in Te Whakarewarewa Thermal Reserve (New Zealand).

water for up to an hour. The time between two eruptions varies from geyser to geyser and can vary between a few minutes to several days, whilst the length of the eruption and the interval between eruptions depends on the quantity of water and the build-up of pressure in the reservoir. Sometimes the interval is nearly constant, like the Old Faithful geyser in Yellowstone Park (USA), which erupts approximately every 45 minutes.

Iceland is renowned for its rugged landscape, its many steaming hot springs and spouting geysers. The word geyser also comes from the Icelandic word 'geysir'.

Iceland is rich in volcanoes, geysers and fumaroles. The island consists of basalt shields dating from the early Tertiary period, alternating with layers of volcanic ash of more recent age. Given its unique location on a volcanic ridge, thermal energy is put to good economic use. Volcanic ridges are always found

▷▷*Electricity is generated in power stations from the hot steam and warm water. Warm water is also used directly to heat buildings. Iceland is richly endowed with this form of energy. Most of the country's electricity is generated from geothermal sources. Houses, factories and greenhouses are thus provided with warmth and electricity.*

on the ocean bed, but in Iceland the volcanic activity has been so intense that the ridge has emerged to lie above sea level, forming the island itself.

Due to the combination of copious amounts of water and underground heat, the country has a considerable number of thermal springs. The steam and warm water from these springs are used to generate electricity and to heat homes, factories and greenhouses. Iceland is so richly endowed with this form of energy that it is able to fulfil its electricity requirements almost wholly from geothermal sources.

Geothermal energy can, in theory, be generated anywhere in the world, because the temperature in the earth's crust increases with depth, and the hot ground water can

Even if geysers are not spouting, they may still bubble. This geyser still has enough energy left to be able to lift a stone.

◁Old Faithful is the best known geyser in the world. It stands in Yellowstone Park (USA) where it was discovered in 1870. Old Faithful spouts some 40,000 litres of water into the air with each eruption. A pause of about three-quarters of an hour follows, during which the underground water reservoir is refilled.

The quantity of water carried into thermal regions depends on the season of the year. In dry periods, the supply drops so much that springs may temporarily dry up. This can also happen if the underground supply system becomes blocked by, for example, the minerals that are being deposited, thus silting up the supply pipes. The blue-grey mud in the springs dries out and cracks. The cracks in the mud form attractive patterns, which are more or less symmetrical.

be used to extract the energy from the lower-lying strata. In places where the ground water circulation encounters physical obstructions, experiments with artificial water flows are being conducted. This is done by pumping water in at great depth and then pumping it up again after it is heated. Unfortunately the geothermal gradient, which is the rise in temperature per 100 metres depth, is only 3 °C. With such a small gradient, the hole that needs to be drilled to obtain water that is sufficiently hot (200 °C) is too deep to be economic. Therefore, it is unlikely that in the coming decades, exploitation of this energy source in places with an average geothermal gradient will be cost-effective.

In volcanic regions, much steeper temperature gradients are found because the hot magma body lies close to the earth's surface. Whilst this is also the case with the volcanic ridges in the centre of the oceans, the thermal sources there lie at too great a depth to be exploited. At present, only those volcanic regions that

lie above sea level can be used for the exploitation of thermal energy.

The first power station to be built using geothermal energy to generate electricity was at Larderello in Italy and dates from 1904. Other places, like Wairakei (New Zealand), Reykjavik,(Iceland) and The Geysers, (USA) followed hesitantly and built their power stations several decades later. In Cerro Prieto (Mexico) there is a power station that is supplied with hot water from an underground reservoir. An impermeable layer of rock above the reservoir prevents the water from escaping, thus creating a

Geysers do not have to spout very high to make an impression. The reflection of sunlight in the water droplets guarantees a wonderful spectacle. Geyser eruptions usually last several minutes.

superheated body of water with a temperature of over 300 °C. If the reservoir is tapped into and the water rises in the pipe, then the pressure reduces causing the water to boil, and turbines can be driven directly by the steam that is formed.

The potential of geothermal energy is enormous. Estimates indicate that this potential is thousands of times greater than the energy that can be extracted from the world's stock of coal and yet globally, geothermal energy is only used on a very modest scale. This is because its extraction and exploitation means taking into account all of the following factors:
  - suitable sources are only available in a limited number of places
  - hot water can only be transported short distances
  - the high concentrations of minerals in the hot water cause corrosion in pipes and joints
  - toxic substances have to be removed.

◁*The Roaring Mountains (Yellowstone Park, US) also lie in a thermally active region. This is not the remnants of the morning mist but is steam rising from the mountains due to the hot materials that lie beneath the rocks. Sometimes the discharge of fumes is so great that the ground begins to shake and a thunderous noise is produced; this explains the name 'Roaring Mountains'.*

At the end of the day, when the air cools, the smoke plumes are easily visible in the evening sun.

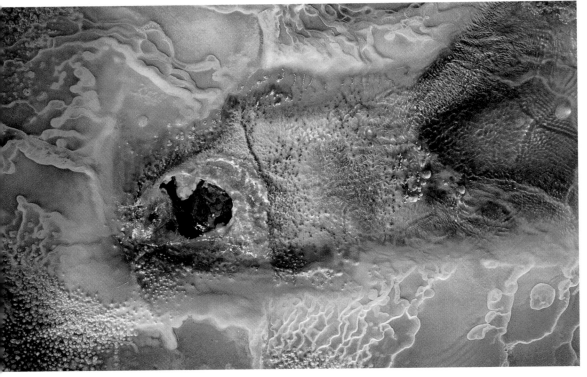

△◁▽ Mud pools and hot springs are created by heat in the earth. Sometimes, however, these phenomena are also due to gases that escape from the ground. The gases create an acid environment that more or less dissolves the ground, which combines with ground water and forms mud pools. If sulphur is present, the mud has a yellow colour and a pungent smell fills the air. The ring-shaped structures occur in spots where the gases rise from the ground.

Moreover, building power stations in volcanic regions is a risky business, because they can be damaged by earthquakes and there is the additional danger of streams of boiling lava or mud. There are also other reasons for deciding not to build power stations; for instance, in Yellowstone Park, if geothermal energy was to be exploited, then the geysers would no longer spout and the tourists would stay away. Yet when the conventional sources of energy are exhausted, other possibilities will have to be investigated. Although at present geothermal energy has limited application possibilities, it may one day be a favourable option, on a par with sun and wind energy.

Other thermal activities

A bubbling pool of mud is also a geothermal phenomenon and it is an amazing sight to see a pool, veiled in fumes, suddenly start to bubble. As with thermal springs, this activity is set in motion by heat transfer from deeper-lying strata. Often part of the bottom of the pool is more or less

The effects of the underground forces come to the surface in this mud pool.

dissolved by the acidic environment, so that, in combination with water, a black porridge-like sludge is formed. The sludge begins to splutter because of the high temperature, but sometimes this is caused by gases that escape from the pool. Oil or graphite brought up from the depths causes the well-known rainbow colour effects in the mud, which are due to the refraction of the light falling on it. If the water supply slows too much during dry periods, or the supply system is blocked, then the pools may also temporarily dry up. Regions containing such pools are dangerous both to man and animals; not only is the ground warm, but noxious gases escape from the water and the water itself is contaminated with heavy metals. Fish

Substances which are brought to the surface in thermal regions can create fascinating effects. In this mud pool in the Te Whakarewarewa Thermal Reserve (New Zealand), beautiful patterns are created by traces of crude oil and graphite, which have formed light-coloured rings in the dark mud.

are unable to survive in these conditions and only certain algae can inhabit the water. Minerals, which are brought to the surface as a result of thermal processes, sometimes form coloured terraces. These grow steadily because the mineral-rich water flowing over them continues to deposit new material. When the hot water meets the air, it evaporates causing the dissolved substances to precipitate out, which then cause the edges of the terrace to

Many different creatures make use of thermal springs; land animals warm themselves in these springs during cold periods. However, a visit to a spring can sometimes end in tragedy, as can be seen in the photograph alongside.

grow slowly higher and to retain more and more water. Where there is a small break in a terrace, the water spills over to a lower-lying terrace. Travertine or sinter terraces are thus created, depending on the temperature and the ground composition. Travertine consists of chalk ($CaCO_3$) and sinter consists of silica (SiO_2).

Warm mud pools in Bolivia.
Bubbles, which are about to burst,
can be clearly seen on the surface.

Unusual colours in the water and on the rocks occur as a result of algae and certain chemical elements (see table below).

The terraces of Mammoth Hot Springs (Yellowstone Park, USA) with their travertine deposits. Hot water, rich in various minerals, flows slowly down over the terraces. As the water evaporates, the minerals are precipitated out.

colour	mineral
white	silicon
yellow/pink	sulphur
orange	antimony
purple	manganese
red/brown	iron oxide

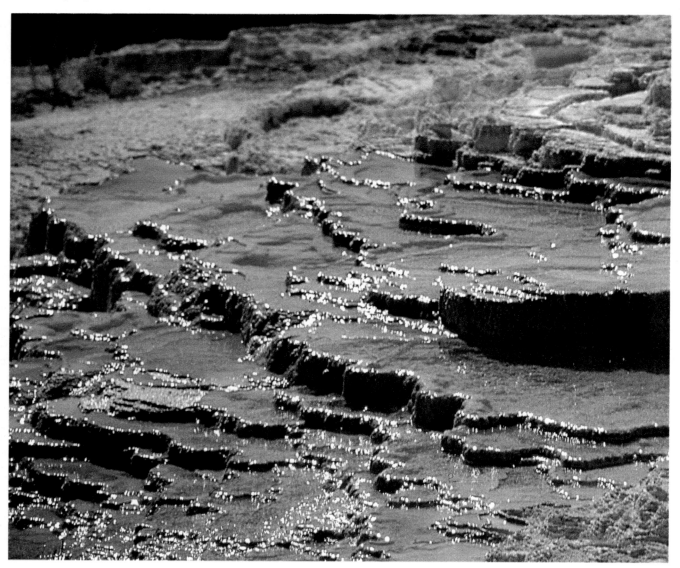

green	arsenic
black	carbon or sulphur

Yellowstone Park, USA

Yellowstone Park, in the state of Wyoming in the United States, is one of the most frequently visited places where thermal activity occurs. There are more than 10,000 hot springs, geysers, mud pools, fumaroles and colourful terraces in the park. Yellowstone Park, the largest thermally active plateau in the world, is the remains of a volcano that erupted half a million years ago,

covering the ground with volcanic material. Calderas have formed as a result of collapses around craters following the eruptions. The largest of these is Yellowstone Caldera, which is 60 kilometres long and nearly 50 kilometres across. Active vulcanism ceased some 500,000 years ago, but some scientists suspect that Yellowstone will, in the very distant future, become volcanically active again.

Terraces grow steadily in size because there is a continuous supply of mineral-rich water. In general, two kinds of deposits are found on terraces: travertine ($CaCO_3$) and sinter (SiO_2), consisting of chalk and silica respectively. The kind of deposit produced depends on the type of mineral in the ground and the temperature of the water.

75

Undersea hot springs

In 1977 geologists made a remarkable discovery. At 'hot spots' on fault lines at a depth of 2,500 metres close to the Galapagos Islands, they discovered warm water welling-up from cracks in the basalt. What surprised the geologists was that around the geysers, there were life-forms that had never been observed before: organisms that drew their energy from the combination of heat rising from the interior of the earth, and from chemosynthesis based on sulphur. It is still unclear how these organisms can spread from one 'hot spot' to another.

A chance discovery made during the drilling of a hole on the Juan de Fuca ridge in 1996, about 200 kilometres off the Canadian coast west of

△▷The hot water and the fumes are rich in minerals and are chemically highly active. A deposit of minerals is formed on the rocks. The various elements provide a range of colours.

The tints of white, yellow, orange and brown are caused by silicon, sulphur, antimony and iron oxide respectively.

Escaping sulphur fumes produce the distinctive smell of rotting eggs.

Vancouver, makes this even less comprehensible. During drilling operations, researchers came upon an area of very high pressure. Volcanic material released from here shot up through the drill hole to tens of metres above the ocean bed. What was remarkable was the colour of the water that gushed out of the drill hole: the cloudy water contained a large amount of a yellowy white substance, which investigations showed to be micro-organisms. A tentative conclusion was drawn: far below the bed of the ocean, organisms live at temperatures of several hundreds of degrees Celsius. One fact is known, that microbes will colonise a new hot undersea spring, but until now it had not been clear where these microbes came from. The discovery of the deep sea geysers with their specific organisms formed the basis for a series of studies on various fault lines in the oceans.

Volcanic processes have played and continue to play an important role in the history of the development of our world. Man makes grateful use of the warmth and energy offered, but the destructive potential of these same underground forces is just as capable of destroying what has been created.

Volcanic region near
Landmannalauger, Iceland.